THE GIANT FISH & JONAH

A BIBLE STORY FROM A UNIQUE PERSPECTIVE

WRITTEN BY AMY LEE CREEL   ILLUSTRATED BY SHANE CREEL

LUCIDBOOKS

THE GIANT FISH AND JONAH

Copyright © 2017 by Amy Creel
Illustrations by Shane Creel

Published by Lucid Books in Houston, TX.
www.LucidBooksPublishing.com

All rights reserved. No part of this publication may be reproduced, stored in a retrieval system, or transmitted in any form by any means, electronic, mechanical, photocopy, recording, or otherwise, without the prior permission of the publisher, except as provided for by USA copyright law.

ISBN 10: 1632961393
ISBN 13: 9781632961396
eISBN 10: 1632961407
eISBN 13: 9781632961402

Special Sales: Most Lucid Books titles are available in special quantity discounts. Custom imprinting or excerpting can also be done to fit special needs. Contact Lucid Books at info@lucidbookspublishing.com.

This book is for our beloved sons, Cullen and Grayson.

Cullen, thank you for inspiring me to finally write my story!

We would like to give our heartfelt thanks to the following people, who were a part of making our publishing dream come true.

Jerry and Shari Creel, *Shane's loving and supportive parents.*
Curt Drouillard, *my sweet daddy*
Julie Drouillard, *my amazing mommy*
Chad, Tawny, Kerigan, and Caston Benoit
Mark and Cindy Carr
The Culver Family
Dr. and Mrs. Paul Drouillard and family
Jared and Tiffany Heathman and family
Fred and Susi Rake
Kelly and Steve Wade
Philbert and Hannah Yau and family
Anthony and Michelle Riley from Creative Grounds Coffee Lounge

And to everyone else who supported us through prayer and our Kickstarter.

THE GIANT FISH & JONAH

A BIBLE STORY FROM A UNIQUE PERSPECTIVE

He was a joyful fish, a gentle fish,
   a very, very silly fish.

He was a loyal fish, an honest fish,
   a very, very thoughtful fish.

Of all the slippery sea creatures,
   he was the kindest fish.

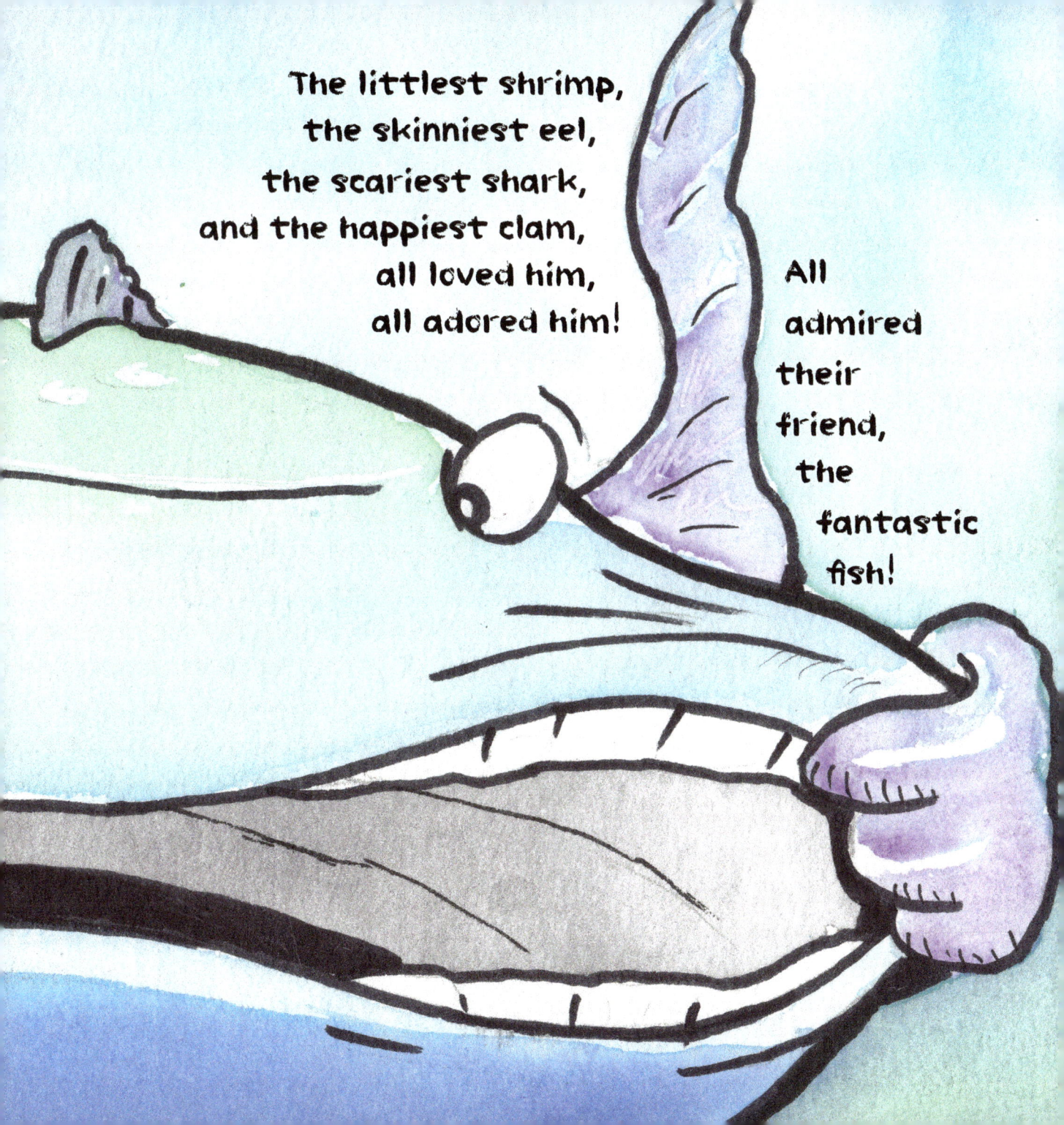

The **super-sized** fish staggered at the sudden sound.

He swam in swift circles, searching the sea for the source. "Who's there?! Whose **big, booming** voice do I hear?"

"There you will see a man named Jonah cast into the sea.

Jonah did not obey me, and now he is trying to hide from me.

I need you to swallow him up!"

Giant Fish
coughed and sputtered on his seaweed sushi.

"But, God! I'm a funny fish! A silly fish! A very, very good fish!

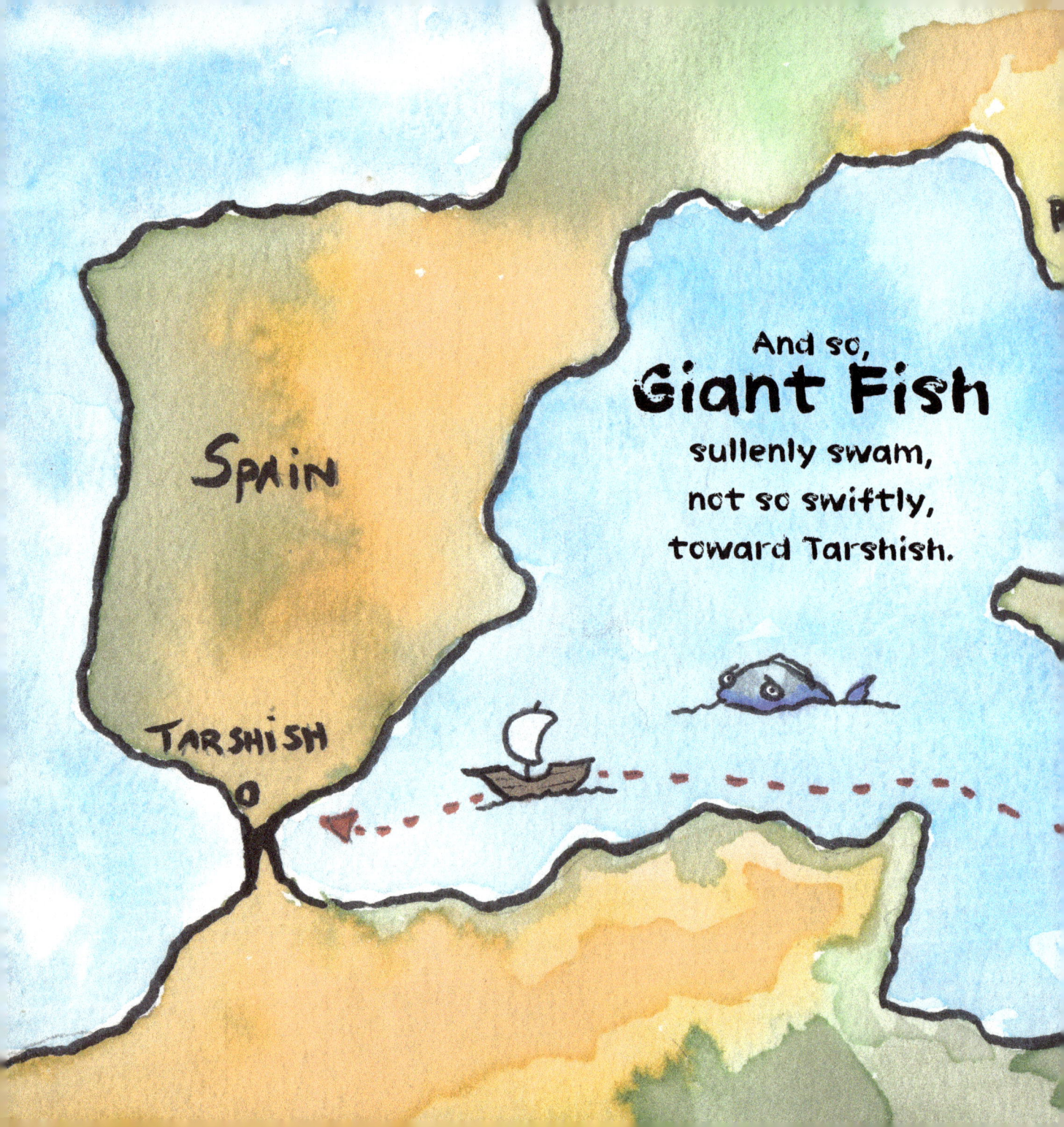

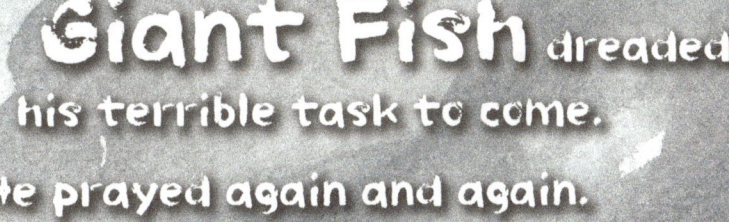

Giant Fish dreaded his terrible task to come. He prayed again and again.

"Why are you asking me to do this, Lord God? I trust you are good but I do not understand!"

On he swam, choosing to obey God, boldly and bravely swishing through the swirling sea.

Giant Fish could hear the men fretting inside the ship.

YAWN

Out came a sleepy stowaway who had somehow been slumbering.

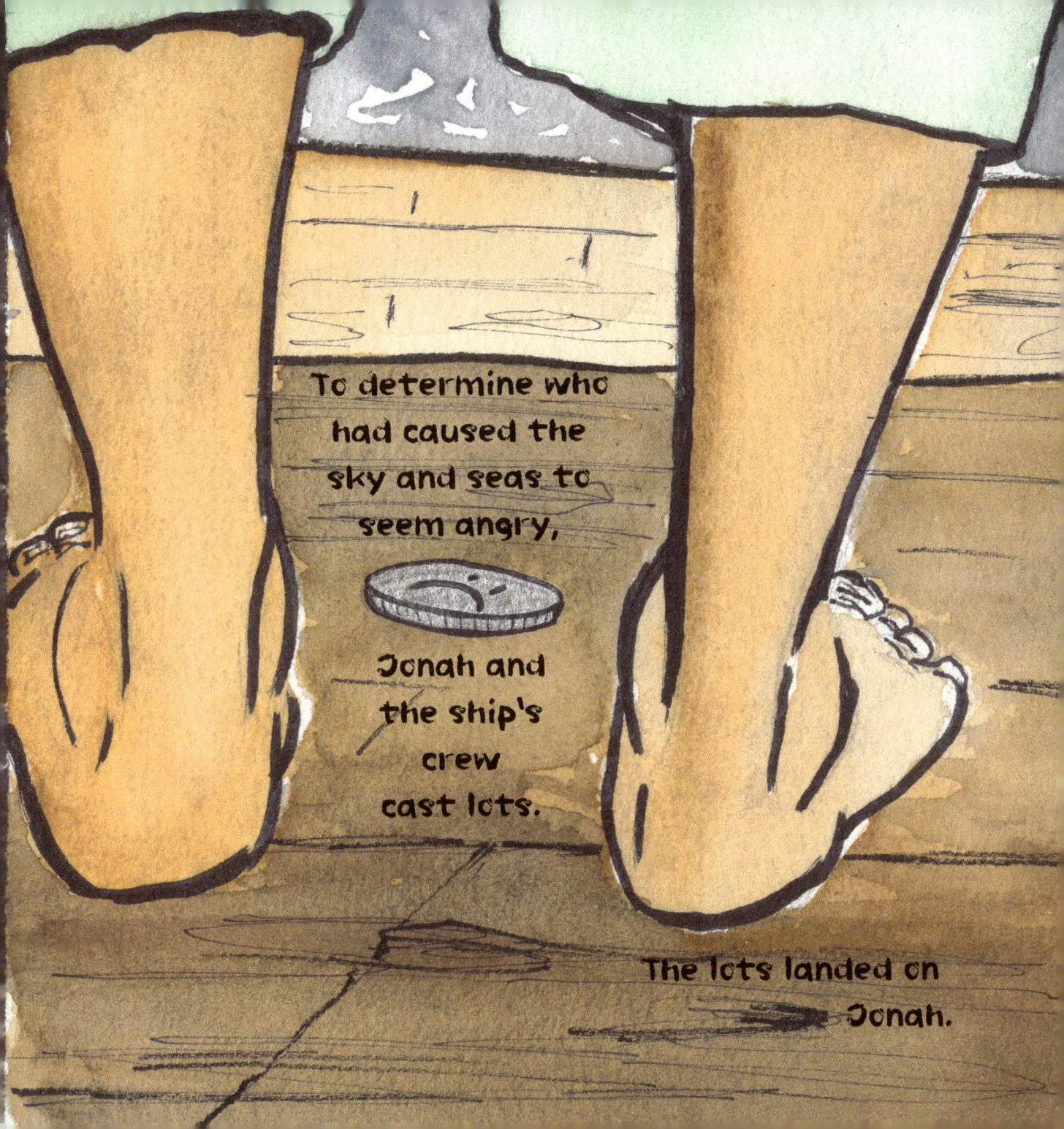

"This terrible tempest is all his fault.

This man runs from God! The God of land and sea.

To save our ship, let's toss him to the salty waters below!"

There was a great big splash as Jonah was thrown into the whipping waves.

He started to
s
 i
  n
   k
    into the
     swirling sea.

Seeing this, **Giant Fish** swam with sudden speed.

He knew this was his purpose,
he knew this was his calling.

The big,
  huge,
    humongous,
      Giant Fish
            knew he must obey.

For three long days, **Giant Fish** held Jonah in his belly.

He held his breath, swam slowly, and hoped not to harm him.

Toting a man in his belly gave him a terrible tummy ache, but he continued to carry the man while waiting to hear a word from God!

For three long nights, **Giant Fish** could not sleep.
From his belly, he could hear the man's muffled prayers.
He heard Jonah sorrowfully say, "Please forgive me."
Jonah was sorry for running from God. His heart had changed.

Giant Fish prayerfully pleaded,
"Oh God, why did I need to swallow this man?
I want to understand. I want to see your purpose.
I know you are good, and so I obey.
God, please show mercy to this man
in my bulging belly."

After the third long night,

Giant Fish woke to the warm rays of a bright and shining sun.
Then at last, he heard God's big, booming voice,

"My faithful fishy fish. You have done well!
You trusted and obeyed even when you did not understand.
You were loyal even when it was hard, even when you were hurting.
Thank you, my dear, sweet, fishy fish.

Giant Fish grew a giant, joyful smile. God was rewarding his loyalty and obedience, and God had forgiven Jonah.

The
big,
huge,
humongous,
Giant Fish
did not like to anger others.
He did not like to hurt others.
And he certainly did not
like to eat others!

And now he did not have to.

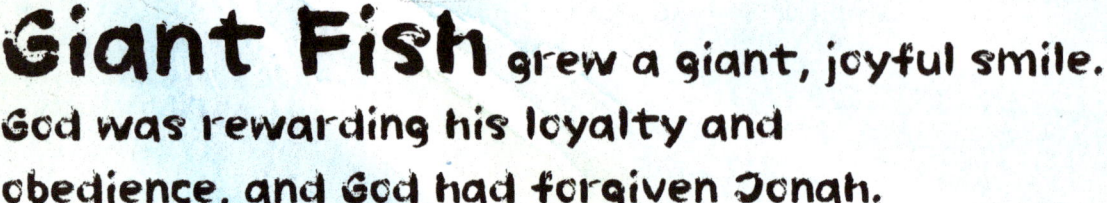

With a silly smile
on his fishy face,
Giant Fish
swam slowly and steadily on his way,
gentle as a jellyfish
so he wouldn't jostle Jonah.

When he approached the sandy shore,
he gave a mighty cough
and safely and soundly
spat
the
man
out.

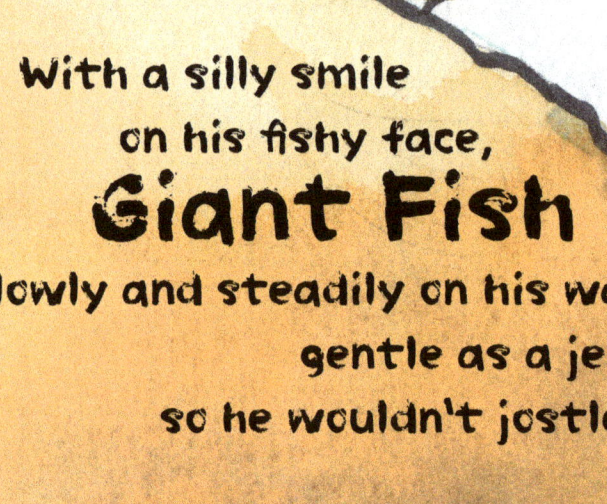

As **Giant Fish** swam away,
he watched from afar.
The man called Jonah wrung out
his clothes, and plucked seaweed from
his sea-drenched beard.

Giant Fish understood that
God had used him to save Jonah's life.
Swallowing him up had saved
the man from sinking.
It had given Jonah's heart
time to change.

Giant Fish

said a prayer of safety for the man as he watched him set off toward Nineveh, which was surely to be a great journey ahead.

It is said that Jonah traveled successfully to the city, where he taught the Ninevite people about God.

Through Jonah, God did great things! Tremendous things!

An entire city learned of God's power and love, all because a **big, huge, humongous** fish trusted and obeyed, becoming part of God's great plan.

Our Marvelous Maker made us into His miraculous masterpiece. He uses us together to fit His perfect plan.

Some of us have hands, some of us have feet, and some have cute, fishy fins.

Discussion & Continued Learning

The Giant Fish & Jonah is a fictional retelling of a Bible story which you can explore further with your child. The Biblical account can be found in the first two chapters of the book of Jonah in the Old Testament.

Discussion Questions:

What were some of the Giant Fish's best qualities?

(Guide your child to the answer of trust, loyalty, kindness and obedience. It's okay if they come up with other traits, too.)

What is Loyalty?

(Loyalty is similar to faithfulness. When we are loyal to someone, we stick with them no matter what. When we are loyal to God, we are faithful to Him and His instructions for our lives.)

⟶ Who is loyal to you?
Who are you loyal to?
How are you loyal to God?

What is Trust?

(Having confidence in someone whom you believe to be good.)

⟶ In your life, who do you trust?

What is Kindness?

(Showing thoughtfulness or being nice to someone.)

⟶ How have you shown kindness to someone?

What is Obedience?

(Following the directions or guidance of someone in authority like a parent or teacher.)

⟶ When are times that you have to obey?
Why is it important to obey?
Has there ever been a time you had to obey God or your parents and you didn't understand why? What happened?

In the story, God rewards Giant Fish for his trust, loyalty, and obedience by letting him spit out Jonah. Sometimes, we may have a big reward for obeying (like cake!) and other times our reward is that God and our loved ones are proud of us!

Can you think of a time that you were rewarded for doing something good?

Jonah chose not to obey God at first, but later came to realize his mistake and asked God to forgive him. God showed Jonah mercy and grace by giving Jonah another chance to do what was asked of him.

Have you ever needed a second chance? Have you ever needed to show mercy to a friend by giving them a second chance?

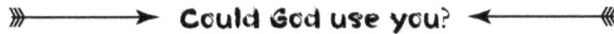

Could God use you?

In the beginning of the story, the fish is described as being loved and adored by his sea creature friends because he is gentle, funny, loyal, and kind. Yet, it is important to note that God values everyone and can use ANYONE to fit his perfect plan. In the Bible, God gives great purpose to ordinary people, weak people, strong people, funny people, serious people, people with many friends, and even people with no friends. YOU are God's perfect creation! God loves and adores YOU, just as you are, and has purpose for your life, too.

God wants a personal relationship with you!

He loves you more than you can possibly imagine. He is good and full of grace and mercy. Even when it feels like you are in the belly of the whale because nothing seems to be going right, God is there. You are God's child, and he has his arms open wide and ready for you. God loved us so much, that he sent his only son, Jesus, to die on a cross to save us from our sins. He said that whoever believes, will have eternal life in Heaven with Him.

If you want to have a personal relationship with God, I encourage you to say a prayer and let God know! You can use the one below as a guide.

God, thank you for dying on the cross for me, so that I can be forgiven of my sins. I trust in you, and want to get to know you more. I need you in my life. Amen.

Continued Learning

➤ Jonah and the sailors cast lots. What does that mean? ◄

Have you ever flipped a coin to make a decision? In sports like football, it is done at the beginning of every game. One player will decide if they want "heads or tails", then the referee flips a coin to determine which team will kick-off first. If the coin lands heads up, then whichever team called "heads" gets to go first.

In Biblical times, the practice of casting lots was common when an unbiased decision needed to be made. That means that decisions were not made based on anyone's opinions, just like in football! Items used to cast lots depended on local customs. It could have been items such as stones, sticks, dice, cards and coins.

Activity: At dinner time, cast lots by flipping a coin to see who helps set the table or cleans the dishes. (Do this with any household duty to help out around the house.)

➤ Where did this journey take place? ◄
(see map in illustrations)

Although it is not mentioned in Giant Fish's story, Joppa is the city where Jonah started his journey. It is located in modern day Joffa, which is by the major city of Tel-Aviv,

Nineveh was the city where Jonah was told to go to by God. It was located in the northern part of modern day Iraq, near the boarder of Turkey. It was on the Tigris River.

Tarshish was the city where Jonah was sailing to when he decided to disobey God. It was in the opposite direction of Nineveh. Tarshish is believed to have been on the western side of the Mediterranean Sea, maybe near southern France.

➤ What kind of fish was big enough to swallow Jonah? ◄

Some Biblical stories are mind boggling! It is important to know that God is ALL POWERFUL! He is not limited by His creation. He can make the impossible become possible. God offers us salvation through faith by trusting in Him, not by completely understanding Him. Thank goodness we don't have to be smart enough to deserve God's love. Phew!

The original words for the Giant Fish in this story are 'ketos' and 'dahg'. They are Greek and Hebrew words, meaning large sea creature. It doesn't translate exactly to whale or fish. There are several types of sea creatures big enough to swallow a human. Some are known for swallowing food whole. That would be important for Jonah! Possibilities include a blue whale, sperm whale, whale-shark, a great white shark, or maybe a species that is extinct.